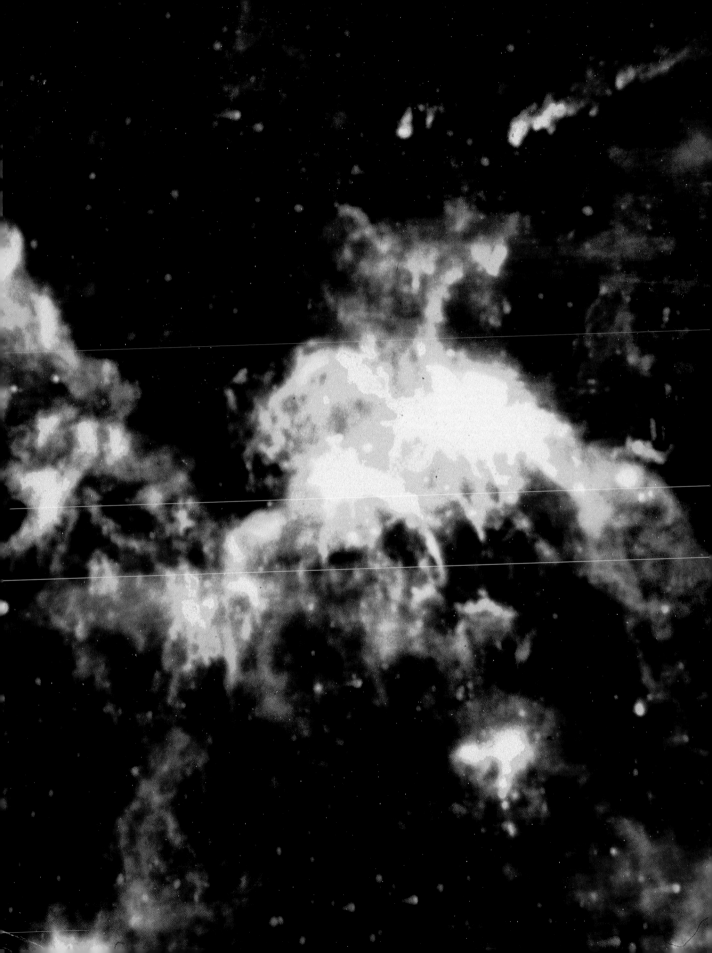

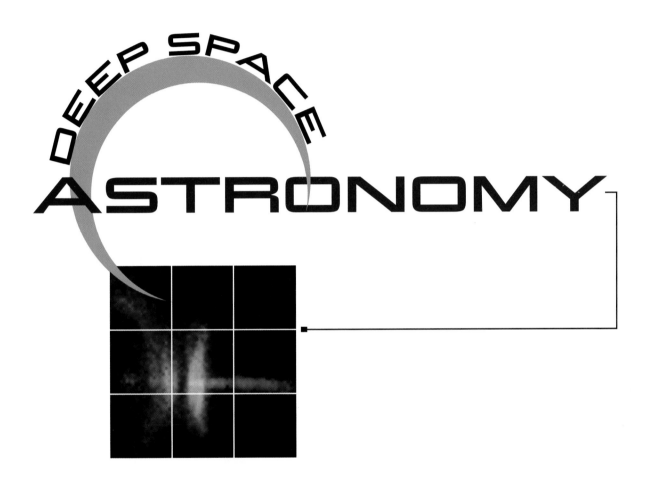

DEEP SPACE

ASTRONOMY

GREGORY L. VOGT

Twenty-First Century Books
Brookfield, Connecticut

Library of Congress Cataloging-in-Publication Data
Vogt, Gregory.
Deep space astronomy/by Gregory L. Vogt.
p. cm.
Includes bibliographical references and index.
Summary: Describes various objects in the universe, where
they are located, and how we measure and observe them from
Earth and with spacecraft.
ISBN 0-7613-1369-9 (lib.bdg.)
1. Outer space–Juvenile literature.   [1. Outer space.
2. Astronomy.]   I. Title.
QB500.22.V6   1999
520–dc21   99-11428   CIP

**Cover photograph courtesy of Jeff Hester and
Paul Scowen (Arizona State University)/NASA**
Photographs courtesy of IRAS: pp. 2, 21 (top, Palomar
Observatory), 22, 43; NASA: pp. 3 (C. Burrows/STScI &
ESA, the WFPC 2 Investigation Definition Team), 5 (J. P.
Harrington and K. J. Borkowski/University of Maryland), 12
(Robert Williams and the Hubble Deep Field Team/STSci),
18, 20 (Akira Fujii), 25, 67 (Raghvendra Sahai and John
Trauger/JPL and the WFPC2 science team), 31, 32, 33, 41,
44 (Jeff Hester and Paul Scowen/Arizona State University), 46
(Peter Garnavich/Harvard-Smithsonian Center for
Astrophysics), 48, 71 (top left, Howard Bond/Space Telescope
Science Institute, Robin Ciardullo/Pennsylvania State
University; top center, Bruce Balick/University of
Washington, Jason Alexander/University of Washington,
Arsen Hajian/U. S. Naval Observatory, Yervant
Terzian/Cornell University, Mario Perinotto/University of
Florence, Italy, Patrizio Patriarchi/Arcetri Observatory, Italy;
top right, Howard Bond/Space Telescope Science Institute,
Robin Ciardullo/Pennsylvania State University; bottom left,
Bruce Balick/University of Washington, Vincent Icke/Leiden
University, The Netherlands, Garrelt Mellema/Stockholm
University; bottom center, Bruce Balick/University of
Washington, Jason Alexander/University of Washington,
Arsen Hajian/U. S. Naval Observatory, Yervant
Terzian/Cornell University, Mario Perinotto/University of
Florence, Italy, Patrizio Patriarchi/Arcetri Observatory, Italy;
bottom right, Howard Bond/Space Telescope Science
Institute, Robin Ciardullo/Pennsylvania State University), 50
(L. Ferrarese/Johns Hopkins University), 54 (John
Bahcall/Institute for Advanced Study, Princeton), 56, 77 (W.
Freedman/Carnegie Observatories and the Hubble Space
Telescope Key Project team,; John Bahcall/Institute for
Advanced Study, Princeton, Mike Disney/University of Wales
and NASA: pp. 70, 74, 75

Published by Twenty-First Century Books
A Division of The Millbrook Press, Inc.
2 Old New Milford Road
Brookfield, Connecticut 06804

Visit our Web site: www.millbrookpress.com

CONTENTS

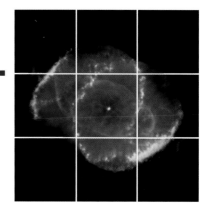

SANDS
OF TIME

Remember the last time you held a handful of beach sand? The grains felt cool and soft as they seeped through your fingers. But the grains were anything but soft. Actually, they were tiny bits of tough minerals eroded by the forces of nature from rocks thousands or millions of years ago. The rocks themselves were forged by planet Earth from the debris left over from the formation of our Sun more than 4.5 billion years ago. And before that, those tiny grains were individual atoms created in the explosions of ancient stars.

A handful of sand can tell the story of the formation of our universe. The sand can also be used to represent the sheer numbers of objects in space. Take stars, for example. How many are there? Sand can help us visualize the answer.

If you had examined one of the sand grains you held closely, you would have noticed that it was sharp and angular and had glassy edges. One grain would be no more than a millimeter across. It would take at least 10 grains set edge to edge to stretch just 1 centimeter (less than 0.5 inch) and 1,000 grains to equal 1 meter (3.28 feet). If you had a box 1 meter wide, 1 meter long, and 1 meter deep (a cubic meter), you would need at least 1 million grains of sand to cover its bottom just one layer deep. It would take 1,000 million grains of sand to fill the box to the brim!

What about a larger box, a school classroom, for example? If the classroom were 10 meters (33 feet) long, 7 meters (23 feet) wide, and 3 meters (10 feet) high, how many grains of sand would it hold? Multiplying those numbers together gives us 210 cubic meters (7,416 cubic feet). If we filled the classroom with sand, it would hold more than 200 billion grains. Try to imagine all those grains. Now, think of the giant collection of stars our Sun resides in. It is called the Milky Way galaxy. By some estimates, the Milky Way holds more than 200 billion stars—the number of grains of sand in a classroom! If you are staggered by that number, prepare yourself for more.

SIZING UP SPACE

Go out on a clear night, and hold up a piece of notebook paper at arm's length toward the Moon. You will find that the Moon fits exactly into one of the paper's three holes. You could also do this with the Sun, but don't. Sunlight will damage your eyes if you look at it too long. You would discover that the Moon and the Sun appear to be the same size in our sky. That is why the Moon can completely cover the Sun during a total solar eclipse.

Even though the Moon and Sun appear to be the same size, their actual diameters are quite different. The Moon's diameter is 3,476 kilometers (2,160 miles), while the Sun is almost 1.4 million kilometers (869,919 miles) across. Then why do these two vastly different-size objects appear the same size to us? The answer is distance. Distance causes small things that are close to look big, and big things that are far away to look small.

Earth, our reference point in this question of sizes, travels in an orbit that averages about 150 million kilometers (93 million miles) from the Sun. An orbit is a nearly circular or elliptical (egg-shaped) path. The Moon, on the other hand, orbits Earth at a distance of approximately 400,000 kilometers (248,548 miles). In other words, the Moon is about 370 times closer to us than the Sun. By a coincidence of nature, the relative sizes and distances of these two bodies balance out so that they look exactly the same size to us in the sky.

Our Earth, the Sun, and the Moon exist in a part of the universe we call interplanetary space. It is the space in which our solar system resides. By human standards, interplanetary space encompasses a huge volume. If we choose to take the orbit of Pluto as its limit, interplanetary space is a sphere 11.8 billion kilometers (7.3 billion miles) in diameter. This sphere is so immense, it took NASA (National Aeronautics and Space Administration) spacecraft like *Voyager I* and *II* nearly two decades to fly from Earth to beyond Pluto's orbit. When they finally traversed that distance they entered a region called interstellar space—the space between the stars. It is a region of our universe containing more than 200 billion stars, which are spread so far apart from one another that even the nearest stars to our Sun appear as mere pinpoints of light.

ASTRONOMICAL METERSTICK

Before venturing any farther into deep space, it is important to understand the concept of astronomical distance. Distances between objects in interstellar space are so great that our usual methods of measuring those distances are almost meaningless. The numbers get so big that they become difficult to work with. For example, the nearest star to us after our Sun is *Alpha Centauri*. Actually, this star is a part of a triple star system, and it is approximately 41,000,000,000,000 (trillion) kilometers (25,000,000,000,000 miles) away. A number with that many digits is not only hard to work with, but even harder to imagine. Furthermore, *Alpha Centauri* is a close star system! The numbers get much bigger. Most of the objects in the universe are billions of times farther away from us than *Alpha Centauri*.

Astronomers get around the big number problem by having a special unit of measurement for distance. The unit is the light-year. It sounds like it is a measurement of time, but it is really an astronomical meterstick. A light-year is the distance that light travels in one year's time. Light moves at the incredible rate of 300,000 kilometers (186,411 miles) per second. By multiplying all the seconds in a year by this speed, we come up with 9.5 trillion kilometers (6 trillion miles). Using this unit instead of ordinary kilometers means that the distance to *Alpha Centauri* can be expressed as a mere 4.3 light-years.

ROOSEVELT'S EYE

Let's go outside again. This time hold a dime out at arm's length in the direction of interstellar space (any direction in the sky). The dime can easily cover two or three stars at a time, even though those stars are probably hundreds of light-years away from each other. If those same stars could be moved farther away from Earth, they would appear even closer to each other.

Now do something harder. Look at the head on the

Here is another way to look at distances in space. Start by drawing an imaginary line between the Sun and Earth. The line would be 150 million kilometers (93 million miles) long. If you could walk at a speed of 5 kilometers (3 miles) per hour continuously, it would take you nearly 3,500 years to walk the distance. Now, let's go farther. A line drawn to Saturn would be about 10 times longer than the line from the Earth to the Sun. A line to the next-nearest star to Earth would extend 30,000 times farther than the line to Saturn. A line drawn from edge to edge across the Milky Way galaxy would be about 20,000 times longer than the line to the next-nearest star. A line drawn across a typical cluster of galaxies in our universe would be about 50 times greater than the line across the Milky Way. Finally, a line drawn across the entire known universe (the part we have been able to see) would reach about 250 times farther than the line across the clusters of galaxies. In other words, multiply the length of a line from the Sun to the Earth by 750,000,000,000,000 (trillion) to get the diameter of the universe! That's about a 2,625,000,000,000,000,000 (quadrillion) year hike!

dime and, in particular, the eye of President Franklin Roosevelt. What objects in space could be covered just by that eye? To see what could lie behind it, look at the picture on page 12. It's not a single picture, but a mosaic of more than 200 pictures combined together to make one scene. The pictures were taken over a 10-day period in December 1995 with NASA's *Hubble Space Telescope* (*HST*). You will learn more about this spacecraft later, but for now just think of it as a large telescope orbiting Earth. The telescope is so powerful and able to see so deeply into space that the part of our universe covered by all these pictures together would fit behind President Roosevelt's eye!

When astronomers processed the pictures into this single scene, they were astounded at the number of objects they saw. Only a few of the objects visible are the stars of

In an area of space covered by the eye of President Roosevelt on the head of a dime held at arm's length, at least 1,500 never-before-seen galaxies were discovered. This picture, the deepest-ever view of a piece of the universe, was taken in December 1995 by the *Hubble Space Telescope*. The picture actually consists of several hundred images that were pieced together. The location of the region is just above the handle and bowl of the Big Dipper constellation. Astronomers think that this picture shows galaxies as they appeared only one billion years after the beginning of the universe. That means that these galaxies could be as much as 14 billion light-years away from Earth.

interstellar space. They show up as bright spots with spikes coming from them. Most of the objects in the mosaic lie at a much greater distance. These are galaxies.

A galaxy is a collection of billions of stars that are tied together by their mutual gravitational pulls and that move around a common center. Our Milky Way galaxy contains more than 200 billion stars, and it is approximately 100,000 light-years in diameter. If the Milky Way were as far from us as the galaxies in this picture, it would look like the spiral-shaped galaxy near the center of the picture.

What we are primarily seeing in this picture is the realm of the galaxies. We call this region intergalactic space. This tiny eye-size piece of deep space reveals thousands of galaxies, each of which contains billions of stars.

What about the rest of deep space? How many Roosevelt eyes would it take to cover it? How many galaxies, stars, and planets would lie behind those eyes? Remember our classroom-size box full of sand grains that equaled the number of stars in the Milky Way galaxy? If we filled all the classrooms on Earth with sand, we would still not have as many grains as there are stars in the universe.

More important than the numbers of objects lying out in deep space is what those objects represent. What are they made up of? How did they form? What processes are at work in them? How do they interact with one another? What great mysteries are waiting there? That is what this book is about.

13

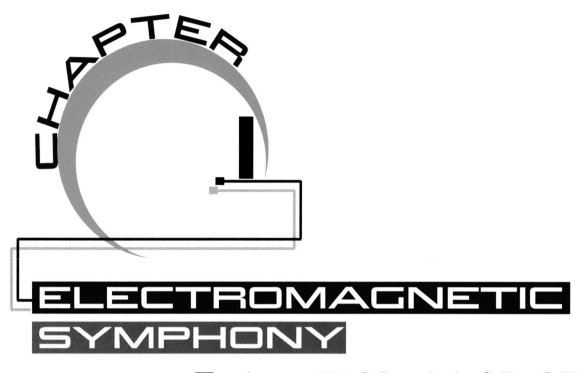

CHAPTER

ELECTROMAGNETIC SYMPHONY

n the year 1609, Italian scientist Galileo Galilei (1564–1642) pointed the first astronomical telescope up to the night sky. Over many months of observations, he discovered four moons circling Jupiter, craters on the Moon, phases of the planet Venus, and spots on the Sun. Galileo's first astronomical telescope, a small tube with glass lenses at each end, magnified distant objects nine times. In effect, his telescope opened a window on the universe.

During the next several hundred years, astronomers built larger telescopes with improved lenses and mirrors. With each new instrument, the window that Galileo opened became wider and deeper. Astronomers looked at the planets and the nearby stars. Then they studied the faint stars much farther away and the fainter stars beyond those. They discovered great fuzzy clouds of gas, now called nebulae, that glowed from the light of stars hidden inside. With more powerful telescopes, some of the nebulae turned out not to be gassy clouds but galaxies of billions of swirling stars.

Regardless of how powerful their telescopes were, astronomers reached limits to what they could do. The window on the universe wasn't as deep or as clear as it could be because their telescopes were fixed to the surface of Earth. Before they could see objects in outer space, astronomers first had to peer through the thick atmosphere of nitrogen and oxygen that surrounds Earth. Water vapor in the air, pollution from forest fires, industrial pollution, automobile exhaust, and dust from volcanic eruptions blotted out some of the light coming to Earth from space. An even greater problem was that the gases in the air itself were not completely transparent. Instead, the atmosphere acted as a filter that permitted only certain forms of light to pass through.

Imagine listening to a concert orchestra in which only the kettledrums and the oboes can be heard. The orchestra could perform a few simple tunes, but most music wouldn't make sense to you. To truly enjoy orchestra music, all the instruments, not only the kettledrums and oboes but also the violins, flutes, cellos, pianos, cymbals, and French horns, have to work. For Earth-bound astronomers, light falling on Earth from outer space is like a symphony played by an incomplete orchestra. Light has many more varieties than the narrow range of seven rainbow colors of red, orange, yellow, green, blue, indigo, and violet (kettledrums and oboes) we can see. There are many other kinds of light—such as radio, X ray, infrared, ultraviolet, and gamma rays—that our eyes are not tuned to.

All of the known forms of light are called the electromagnetic spectrum. To understand this spectrum, we must first understand the nature of light. Light is not a simple

The electromagnetic spectrum is more than just the domain of astronomers. It is a handy thing to have around. All of our radio and television programs depend upon radio waves for transmission. Mobile telephones and toy racing cars also need radio waves. Microwave radiation is used to cook food, transmit telephone calls, and in computer data links. Infrared light keeps our french fries warm and sends our channel selections from the remote control to the television set. Visible light is what we see with. Ultraviolet light tans our skin. In the right amounts, ultraviolet light can be used to treat some diseases, but too much ultraviolet can damage our skin and lead to cancer. X rays are useful in medical diagnosis. Gamma rays can be used by doctors to destroy diseased cells.

phenomenon. It is a form of energy that travels at 300,000 kilometers (186,411 miles) per second through the vacuum of space. The energy in light behaves both like particles and like waves at the same time. The particle nature of light can be observed with a solar-powered pocket calculator. Light strikes the solar cell on the calculator like a rain of particles, each carrying a bit of energy. The energy drives an electric current from the cell through the calculator and back.

As waves, light is similar to water rolling up on a beach. Water waves have a high point called a crest and a low point called a trough. You can stand on the beach and determine the frequency of the waves by counting how many waves strike the beach over a period of time. For example, if a wave strikes the beach every 10 seconds, the frequency is 0.1 or 1/10th. Frequency is the number of waves that reach a reference point each second. If a different set of waves, traveling at the same speed, strike the beach one every second, the frequency is 1.

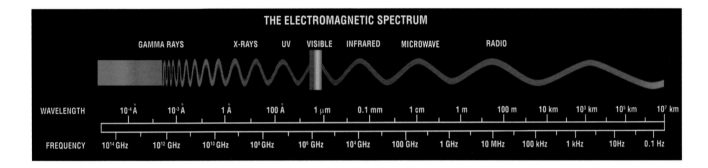

The difference between waves with a frequency of 0.1 and 1 is the wave property called wavelength. A wavelength is the distance between one wave crest and the next one (or one wave trough and the next one). You will observe that the waves with a frequency of 0.1 are very long compared with waves with a frequency of 1. Since both waves travel at the same speed, it is their wavelengths that determine how often (frequency) the waves strike the beach.

Compared with water waves, the wavelengths of visible light are extremely short. Fifty of these waves strung crest to trough would just cross the thickness of a piece of kitchen plastic wrap. This gives them a frequency of about 600 billion per second! This may seem like a lot, but gamma rays have a frequency many million times more per second.

Light waves of all kinds travel at the same speed. It is their wavelengths that determine their frequency. Gamma rays, at the small end of the electromagnetic spectrum, can have wavelengths smaller than the thickness of an atom. Radio waves, at the other end of the electromagnetic spectrum, have wavelengths ranging from a few centimeters to several kilometers. Across the electromagnetic spectrum, frequencies range from the hundreds per second (radio waves) to billion trillions per second (gamma rays).

What does the wave nature of light mean to astronomers? The answer is information. Each specific wavelength carries a bit of information about the body that created it. If you have a Slinky®, you can illustrate this for yourself. Have someone hold one end of the Slinky® while you hold the other. Stretch it out across a long tabletop. Have your partner begin shaking the Slinky® from side to side. You will immediately observe waves traveling through the Slinky® to you. With a meterstick and a watch, you can measure the wavelength and frequency of the waves. Now have your partner begin shaking the Slinky® very rapidly. You will observe that wavelengths get shorter and their frequency increases. Furthermore, your partner will report that high-frequency waves take much more energy to make than low-frequency waves. This means that you can tell, on the receiving end of the waves, about the energy it took to make the waves reaching you just by looking at their frequency.

How does this apply to space observations? Objects in space, like stars, nebulae, and galaxies, send out many forms of light all at the same time. They emit visible light, radio waves, X rays, and so on. If we collect those emissions, we can tell about the objects that created them. Each kind of light is produced by different processes and at different temperature ranges. Thus, light waves carry stories for astronomers to interpret.

STORIES IN LIGHT

Radio Waves

What do radio waves tell us? Radio waves have the lowest energies and tell us about low-energy objects in space, such as cool clouds of gas and dust (nebulae) that will eventually condense to form new stars. The temperatures of these objects range from close to absolute zero (the coldest anything can get) to about the freezing point of water (32°F, or 0°C). Radio waves are emitted in a variety of ways. One way is for atoms to collide with other atoms and begin spinning. In time, the spinning atoms release a radio wave, and the loss of energy causes them to slow down. These collisions are very common in nebulae. Most radio waves are able to penetrate Earth's atmosphere and reach Earth's surface, so astronomers can study them without traveling to outer space. Huge dish-shaped radio telescopes and networks of smaller radio telescopes are mounted in many remote locations on Earth to capture the waves from low-temperature events. Remote locations help shield radio telescopes from interference from radio signals generated on Earth.

Microwaves

Microwaves are a form of radio waves that exist on the higher frequency end of the electromagnetic spectrum next to infrared radiation. The universe is relatively quiet in the microwave range, and few spacecraft are tuned to it. Microwave radiation does provide information about the remnant radiation left over from the beginning of the universe.

Infrared Radiation

Infrared radiation from space is much harder to capture. Most of this brand of light is filtered out by moisture in

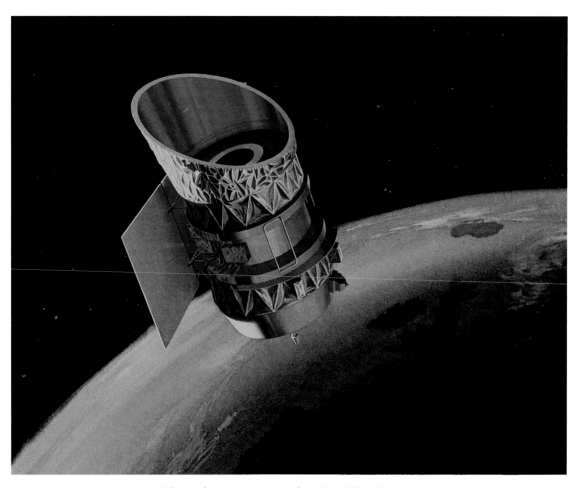

The *Infrared Astronomical Satellite (IRAS)* was constructed by the United States, the United Kingdom, and the Netherlands and launched into space in 1983. During its life span, *IRAS* made infrared observations of 20,000 galaxies, 130,000 stars, and 90,000 other space objects and star clusters.

Earth's atmosphere. Some of it does reach down a short way into Earth's upper atmosphere, where it can be captured by instruments on mountaintops and on high-flying airplanes and balloons. But the information can be confusing because the atmosphere itself is also a source of infrared radiation. Infrared radiation is useful for learning about space objects existing at a range from very low temperatures to room temperature. With infrared light coming from space, we see dusty regions that are warmed by nearby stars and dying stars that are ejecting shells of matter. Infrared radiation is produced when tiny dusty particles absorb light energy from stars and warm up as a result. The particles slowly cool off by emitting infrared rays.

Visible Light

Visible light, the next most energetic band in the electromagnetic spectrum, is able to penetrate Earth's atmosphere and reach the surface. Its trip is not easy. Some visible light is blocked by clouds and various forms of natural and human-made pollution and distorted by air currents. Daylight brightens the atmosphere and obscures the stars. To minimize visible light–collection problems, observato-

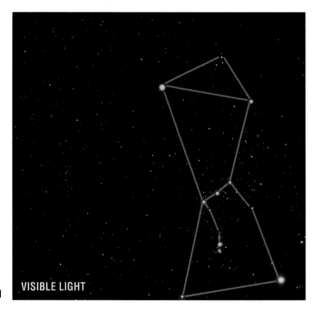

VISIBLE LIGHT

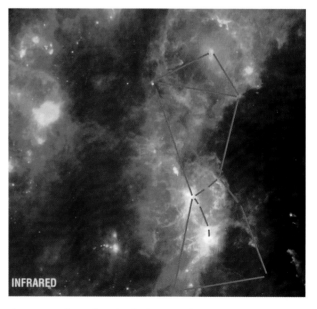

INFRARED

The difference between the visible light view of space and the view in infrared is shown in this pair of pictures of the constellation Orion. Newly forming stars are difficult to see in the visible light view but stand out in the infrared view taken by the *Infrared Astronomical Satellite*. The orange and red glowing clouds between the stars are interstellar dust and gas.

Each kind of radiation in the electro-magnetic spectrum has a different story to tell astronomers. The visible light Andromeda galaxy picture at top left was taken with the 500-centimeter (200-inch) Mt. Palomar Observatory telescope in southern California. The galaxy, near the constellation Andromeda, is about 2.2 million light-years from Earth. The picture at bottom left is also the Andromeda galaxy, but it was taken with the *Infrared Astronomical Satellite*. The hottest areas (greatest amount of infrared radiation emitted) are shown as yellow and red. The cooler regions are blue.

ries are often placed on mountaintops in remote locations, and viewing is restricted to nighttime.

Visible light is an important messenger from space. It represents objects and events operating at the temperature range of the surface of the Sun—about 5,500°C (9,930°F). Visible light is produced when atoms are energized by collisions with other atoms or when atoms are struck by light produced by other atoms. Electrons circling the nuclei of these atoms receive this energy and change their orbits momentarily. As these electrons return to their normal orbits, they release a spark of visible radiation. Astronomers use the information contained in visible light to study the billions of ordinary stars in the Milky Way galaxy and to study other galaxies throughout the universe to learn how they evolve and how they consume their nuclear energy.

Stars essentially are nuclear furnaces in which atoms of hydrogen are combined at very high temperatures and pressures to form atoms of helium. A small amount of the mass of the hydrogen, less than one percent, is converted into energy that we see as light and feel as heat. The process is called thermonuclear fusion. It's what happens in a hydrogen bomb when it detonates. Our Sun, as an example of an average star, converts about 5 million tons of its mass to energy every second through thermonuclear fusion.

Another story that visible light tells astronomers is the chemical composition of stars and nebulae, the star temperatures, and even how bodies in space are moving in relation to one another. Those aspects of visible light will be discussed later.

Ultraviolet Light

Just beyond visible light in the electromagnetic spectrum is ultraviolet light. Although most of this form of light is filtered out by the atmosphere, small amounts still reach Earth's surface. Ultraviolet light is produced in the same way that visible light is produced. This form of light gives astronomers information similar to that given by visible light, only at temperatures ranging into the hundreds of thousands of degrees.

X rays

At even smaller wavelengths and at higher temperatures than ultraviolet light are X rays. X rays are produced in various ways by highly energetic atomic particles interacting with one another. They tell the story of violent events in space such as how the strong gravity of one star can rip away the atmospheres of nearby stars with weaker gravitational pull. X rays reveal matter in the temperature range of 30 million degrees Celsius (86 million degrees Fahrenheit).

Gamma Rays

At the opposite end of the electromagnetic spectrum from radio waves are gamma rays. Gamma rays are the mes-

■ Once a giant reddish star 8,000 light-years away, the Hourglass Nebula formed as the star explosively shed layer upon layer of gas into outer space. Today, we see these layers as intersecting rings of gas—nebulae. Ultraviolet light from the remainder of the star causes the gas rings to glow.

Astronomers refer to nebulae like this one as planetary nebulae because they are disk-shaped and look like planets when seen through their Earth-bound telescopes. With the *Hubble Space Telescope*, the true appearance of this nebula was revealed.

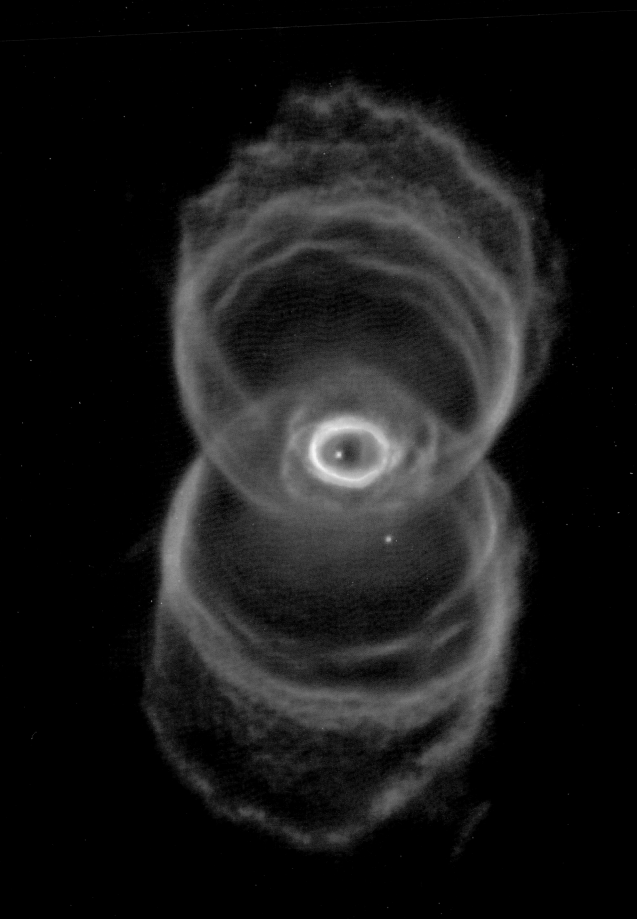

THE TIME MACHINE

Because of the vast distances in space, astronomers have an enormously useful tool at their disposal—a kind of time machine, you might say. If an astronomer looks at a star that lies 100 light-years away, the light that is seen is 100 years old. The star looks as it did 100 years ago. If the star is 10,000 light-years away, the astronomer sees the star as it looked 10,000 years ago. By looking farther and farther into space, astronomers are able to step backward in time.

This becomes useful when they look at similar objects. For example, if they see a particular kind of galaxy one billion light-years away and a similar galaxy twice as far away, they have a kind of photo album. The picture of the first galaxy shows how it looked one billion years ago, and the second picture shows how it looked two billion years ago. The difference between the two pictures gives astronomers information about how galaxies evolve over time.

sengers of the most violent events in the universe, such as the destruction of stars in explosions called novae and supernovae. Novae occur when a star blows off a shell of matter from its surface into outer space. The star grows intensely brighter for a short time until the shell cools down and dissipates and the star returns to its normal brightness. Supernovae are much more powerful. The core of the star detonates and converts its gases into energy while leaving behind a cinder of heavier elements such as iron. It was in supernovae billions of years ago that much of the matter that makes up the Earth was created. That means the atoms in the book you are holding and your hands and the rest of your body were created in the ancient detonation of stars. Gamma rays represent cataclysmic events as hot as 10 billion degrees Celsius (50 billion degrees Fahrenheit).

LISTENING TO
THE CELESTIAL
ORCHESTRA

To learn about the wide range of phenomena in outer space, astronomers need to collect all the different forms of light emitted from those phenomena to fully understand what they are looking at. While some of this information can be collected from Earth-based observatories, the rest has to be collected in outer space.

The point of studying all the radiations of the electro-magnetic spectrum is that taken together they represent a kind of family album. Each wavelength band is like a page in the album and tells a different part of the story. Studying the whole of the electromagnetic spectrum is like listening to an orchestra in which every instrument can be clearly heard. The music makes sense and is beautiful. The problem for astronomers is how to hear all the instruments. Since all the bands do not reach Earth's surface, astronomers have to send their telescopes into outer space.

CHAPTER 2

ASTRONOMY SPACECRAFT

I n the early days of exploring outer space with rockets, the late 1940s and early 1950s, just getting into space was a tremendous challenge. Many rockets exploded on the launchpad or flew off course and had to be destroyed. It was a frustrating time for rocket scientists, but each failure taught them important lessons, and their rockets improved. By the mid-1950s powerful rockets were becoming reliable. Their aim was not just to reach outer space but to put a satellite in orbit.

The idea for accomplishing this was simple. Launch a rocket above Earth's atmosphere and then aim it parallel to the ground. If the rocket achieves the right speed, it will coast around the world when its engines stop firing. The rocket would actually be falling, but it would be going forward at the same time. Whenever an object is traveling forward as it is falling, the object traces a curved path. With the right speed the curved path of the rocket would match the shape of the Earth, and an orbit would be achieved.

Scientists in the Soviet Union were the first to get it right. On October 4, 1957, they launched *Sputnik*, the first artificial Earth satellite. On January 31, 1958, *Explorer 1* was launched by the United States. The space age had begun.

THE FIRST SPACE EXPLORERS

It wasn't long before many rockets began carrying scientific satellites into space. Most of the early satellites investigated the near-Earth environment for radiation and micrometeoroid density. Micrometeoroids are tiny bits of space rock and dust traveling through space at speeds of many kilometers per second. A collision between a micrometeoroid and a satellite could cause serious damage to the satellite. The information these satellites obtained was important when the time came for humans to travel into space. Scientists needed to know that the spacecraft they developed would be safe.

Later, satellite instruments were used to look out into the solar system. Astronomers finally had the solution to the problem of not being able to study the entire electromagnetic spectrum from Earth's surface. Send telescopes into space!

Among the first of the astronomy satellites were the *Orbiting Solar Observatory I* (*OSO I*), launched in 1962, and the *Orbiting Astronomical Observatory I* (*OAO I*), launched in 1966. *OAO I* suffered battery problems and failed shortly after reaching space. *OAO II* replaced it two years later.

These early space observatories carried detectors to measure ultraviolet radiation, X rays, and gamma rays—parts of the electromagnetic spectrum that do not pass through Earth's atmosphere. From the beginning, astronomers realized that satellites and ground-based telescopes could work together. A satellite would detect some mysterious object strongly emitting X rays, for example, and ground-based telescopes would be aimed in the same direction to see what visible light it was putting out. The reverse approach was used as well. A strong visible light emitter, such as a distant galaxy, would be located by a ground-based telescope and then studied by the satellites in space.

DISCOVERY MACHINE

On December 2, 1993, the space shuttle *Endeavour* rocketed into space. The crew of seven astronauts guided their orbiter to a rendezvous with a huge astronomy spacecraft called the *Hubble Space Telescope*. The spacecraft was named for astronomer Edwin P. Hubble (1889–1953). In the early part of the twentieth century, Hubble proved that some of the faint nebulae that astronomers were wondering about were actually very distant galaxies like our own Milky Way galaxy.

After capturing the telescope in *Endeavour*'s payload bay, four of the crew, working in alternating shifts of two, donned spacesuits and stepped out into space. Their goal was to replace certain instruments on the telescope with upgraded versions and to install new solar panels. The *Hubble Space Telescope* had been launched by the space shuttle *Discovery* three years earlier. It was going to extend the work that Galileo had started with his telescope nearly 400 years earlier. It was going to open up new windows on the universe.

Space shuttle astronaut Story Musgrave, attached to the end of a robot arm, prepares to work on the *Hubble Space Telescope*, while Jeffrey Hoffman moves about the payload bay. Over a period of a few days, various instruments and even the solar panels for the spacecraft would be replaced.

Repair and servicing of the *Hubble Space Telescope* was a team effort. Starting with Richard O. Covey, mission commander (red shirt) and going clockwise are pilot Kenneth D. Bowersox, mission specialist Claude Nicollier, payload commander F. Story Musgrave, and mission specialists Jeffrey A. Hoffman, Kathryn C. Thornton, and Thomas D. Akers. The spacewalkers are wearing striped shirts. While working on the telescope Nicollier operated the shuttle's robot arm, and Covey and Bowersox controlled the vehicle.

Flying above Earth's atmosphere, the *Hubble*'s 2.4-meter (7.9-foot)-diameter mirror would be able to see ten times deeper into the universe than the best Earth-based telescopes. Mission scientists predicted that the pictures it would radio back to Earth would astound the world. The telescope was going to be so powerful that it could separate the two headlights of a car at a distance of 5,000 kilometers (3,107 miles)! It didn't work out that way. A mistake was made, and the telescope's giant mirror was ground to the wrong shape. The error, equal to about one-fiftieth the thickness of a human hair, was tiny—but it caused the images of distant objects in space to be slightly blurred. The pictures the telescope did send to Earth were

The Sun's surface is a violent place. It seethes with eruptions that form great expanding arches of glowing gas, sometimes hundreds of thousands of kilometers above the surface. The temperature of the Sun's surface is about 6000°C (10,832°F), considerably cooler than the core temperature. Some areas of the surface periodically have dark spots. The spots look darker than the rest of the surface because they are a few hundred degrees cooler and don't glow as brightly.

Above the surface is a huge atmosphere of very thin gas that extends out millions of kilometers. The shape of the Sun's atmosphere, as well as many of its surface features, are controlled by a powerful magnetic field.

The Sun can be thought of as an average star. Its size and temperature are middle of the road. This is good for the Earth because stars like our Sun consume their nuclear fuel at a slow, steady rate. The Sun is thought to be about 5 billion years old, and it is estimated to last another 5 billion years before running out of fuel!

Deep-space views from the *Hubble Space Telescope* and other astronomy spacecraft reveal many stars like our Sun, but also many others that are quite different. Space observatories have captured stars in various stages of growth from their beginnings in gaseous nebulae to their final death throes in supernovae.

STELLAR NURSERIES

In 1983 the *Infrared Astronomical Satellite* took infrared pictures of stellar nurseries in the Great Nebula of the constellation Orion. The giant gas cloud has areas where the gas is more densely packed than in others. Because of gravity, these dense pockets are drawing the gas inward

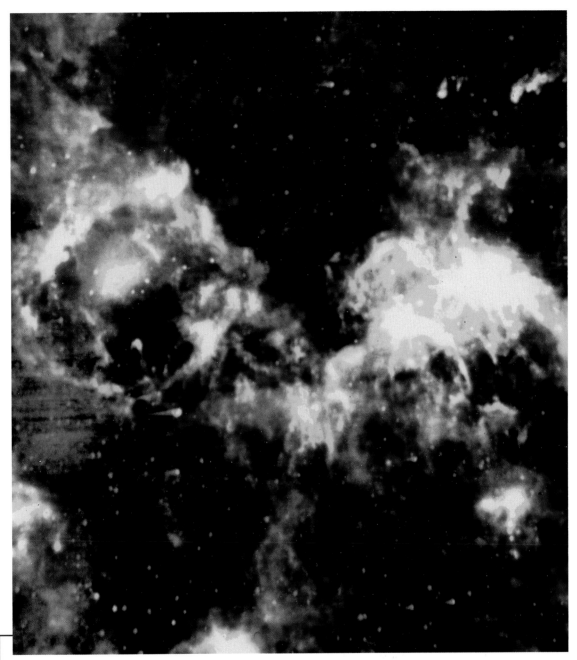

Located in the constellation of Orion, portions of the gas and dust in this nebula are condensing into new stars. As the gas and dust condense into clumps, the gravitational attraction of the clumps grows and causes more gas and dust to fall inward. Eventually the clumps will become star-size and their nuclear furnaces will kick into action. This picture was taken with the *Infrared Astronomical Satellite.*

The fingerlike projections at the upper tip of this nebula in the constellation Serpens hide newly forming stars (EGGs). The gas in this nebula is mostly hydrogen. When enough hydrogen accumulates in the new stars, thermonuclear fusion will begin, and the stars will emit their own light. The remaining nearby gas of the nebula will be blown away by the star's energy.

and in time will have enough mass to ignite their nuclear furnaces to become stars.

The *Hubble Space Telescope* also captured star formation in the Eagle Nebula, some 7,000 light-years away in the constellation Serpens. Dense small knots of gas, called evaporating gaseous globules (EGGs), harbor newborn stars. As the stars ignite, the remainder of the gas forming the globules is blown away by their growing heat and brightness.

SUPERNOVA 1987A

The beginning of a star is a relatively quiet event. The end of a star can be spectacular. The *Hubble Space Telescope* has been used repeatedly to monitor the progress of a star that exploded in a supernova in 1987. The star is named supernova 1987A because it was the first supernova to be observed that year. It is located 169,000 light-years away in the Large Magellanic Cloud—a satellite galaxy of our own Milky Way galaxy.

The powerful magnification of the *HST* revealed the exploding star had a light-year–wide ring of glowing gas surrounding it. Astronomers think that the ring was shed by the star 20,000 years ago in a smaller explosion and has been expanding ever since. According to one theory, the star that created the supernova was actually a binary system, or pair of stars. The two stars, one large and one small, could have merged to become one large blue star while shedding some of their gas to form the ring.

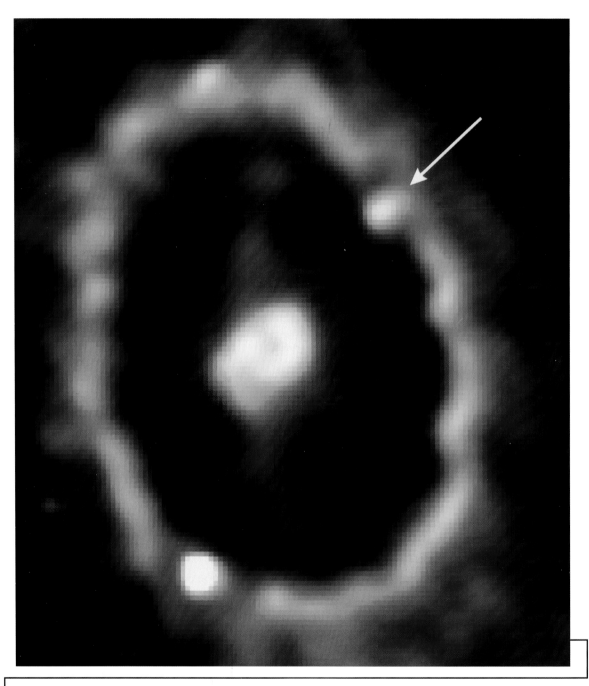

■ Continued observation of the ring that formed around the star after it exploded to form Supernova 1987A has shown the brightness of the ring beginning to fade.

In 1998, a knot in the ring (see arrow) began glowing more brightly when it was hit by a new blast wave coming from the star.

Eleven years after the supernova erupted, *HST* images enabled astronomers to witness the collision of an outward-rushing shock wave from the supernova with the older ring. The explosion shock wave is traveling outward from the supernova at a speed of 65 million kilometers (40 million miles) per hour! It slammed into a 160-billion-kilometer (100-billion-mile) knot of gas in the old ring. The collision caused temperatures in the knot, normally in the range of a few thousand degrees, to jump to 550,000 degrees Celsius (1 million degrees Fahrenheit).

Astronomers had expected to see the collision because they had spotted an outward-moving shock wave several years earlier. Radio and infrared telescopes detected the shock wave as it began colliding with invisible gas deep inside the ring. Continued observation of supernova 1987A and its shock wave will help astronomers learn more about the structure of the ancient ring and the star that created it. It is expected that the continuing outward expansion of the shock wave will cause the entire ring to glow as brightly as the knot.

PLANETARY
NEBULAE

As astronomers scan deep space with their telescopes, they occasionally come across small gas clouds that resemble disks of planets. The English astronomer William Herschel (1738–1822) was the first to see these objects, which he thought resembled the planet Uranus. For that reason Herschel called the objects planetary nebulae. The name has stuck even though distance measurements taken later indicated that the objects were well outside our solar system. With closer examination afforded by larger telescopes, planetary nebulae were revealed to be stars that have shed

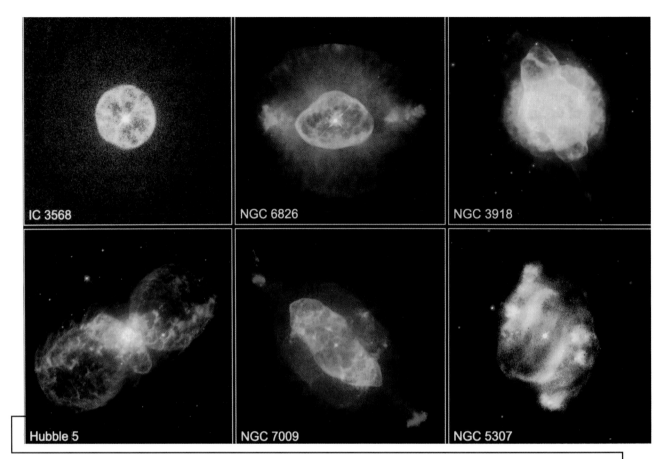

IC 3568

NGC 6826

NGC 3918

Hubble 5

NGC 7009

NGC 5307

Hubble Space Telescope **pictures of planetary nebulae reveal objects that could be mistaken for works of modern art. These six planetary nebulae show spherical, eye, spiral, and butterfly shapes. Each has originated from an ancient Sun-like star that shed its outer layers of gas, while its core contracted to become a hot white dwarf star.**

one or more layers of gas. Ultraviolet radiation emanating from the star inside the layers causes the gas in the layers to glow in visible light that can be seen in telescopes. When their true nature became known, astronomers reasoned that the gas layers would be shed as spherical shells that would gradually grow larger until they dissipated into space. Because the gas layers were somewhat transparent, the star in the middle of the nebula could be seen, while the edges of the nebula looked thicker because of the angle they were viewed at. This gives some planetary nebulae the appearance of ringed stars. When the *Hubble Space Telescope* was used by astronomers to study planetary nebulae, astronomers discovered that many were not spherical at all. They took on butterfly, football, eye, and even rocket-engine–exhaust shapes.

Stars that create planetary nebulae are like our Sun. By looking at them, we get an idea of what will happen to our Sun in 5 billion years or so. Toward the end of the life span of Sunlike stars, their cores begin contracting and getting hotter. While this happens, the gas from the outer part of the star expands 200 times, and the star becomes a red giant. Later the red giant fades. Its remaining gas continues to travel outward. The core of the star collapses until it becomes a white dwarf. The hot white dwarf releases intense ultraviolet light that strikes the outward-moving gas and causes it to glow in visible light. The colors seen in the nebula come from the different gases that are present. Red is produced by hydrogen gas, green by oxygen, and blue by helium. The gas traveling at different speeds in different directions, and the gravity from nearby stars, distort the nebula to produce bizarre shapes.

BLACK HOLES

The life of a star is a contest between gravity and nuclear fusion. The gases that make up a star produce a tremendous gravitational attraction that drags that matter inward on itself. The tighter the matter is packed, the stronger the gravitational force; and the stronger the force, the more it pulls on itself. Without something to balance this inward force, a star can fall inward on itself until it is infinitely small.

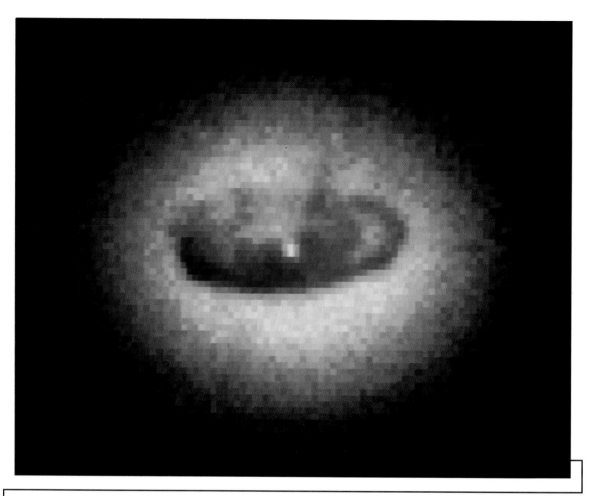

■ The *Hubble Space Telescope* had detected a black hole near the center of a galaxy 100 million light-years away. The galaxy, NGC 4261, is found in the direction of the constellation Virgo. What the *HST* discovered was a spiral-shaped disk of gas and dust 800 light-years wide falling into a black hole located at its center. From calculations of the speed of the matter swirling into the black hole, astronomers believe that the black hole is 1.2 billion times more massive than our Sun. The astronomers have speculated that the source of the gas and dust, enough to make 100,000 stars like our Sun, is a remnant of a small galaxy that fell into NGC 4261.

The outward-balancing force is the nuclear fusion reaction that converts some of the matter of the star into energy. Like air that expands when it is warm, nuclear fusion expands the star.

Throughout most of the life of a star, gravity and nuclear fusion battle it out, producing a star that remains more or less constant in size. Eventually, however, the star runs out of nuclear fuel, and gravity finally wins. What happens then depends upon what kind of star it was. Stars like our Sun may temporarily expand their outer layers so that they become giant red stars. In time the last of the hydrogen and helium is consumed, and the light of the expanding layers fades away. The remainders of these stars collapse inward on themselves and produce hot cores of densely packed matter called white dwarfs. Smaller in diameter than Earth, white dwarfs weigh about as much as 100,000 Earths combined. A single handful of the matter of a white dwarf would weigh as much as a 747 jet aircraft. Over billions of years, the white dwarfs cool and stop giving off light. They then become black dwarfs.

Red giant stars, about 10 times more massive than our Sun, have a more dramatic ending. They may detonate in a titanic explosion, as did the star that became supernova 1987A. The force released would be about the same as that produced by a mass of TNT equal to one trillion Earths exploding all at once!

The remnants of stars that have become supernovae become extremely dense objects called neutron stars or even denser black holes. Which one depends upon how much matter remains. If the remnants are between about 1.2 and 3 solar masses (1.2 to 3 times the mass of the Sun), gravity causes them to crash inward on themselves until they are only about 10 kilometers (6 miles) in diameter. Then they become neutron stars consisting only of neutrons. Neutrons are particles found in the nucleus of the atom. Neutron stars are so dense that a chunk the size of a sugar cube would weigh about 50 million kilograms (about 110 million pounds) on Earth. The high density and small diameter of neutron stars causes them to have a

One of the major questions of astronomy is how the universe began. Many astronomers think they have the general answer to the question, although many details are yet to be worked out. The explanation is part of what is called the Big Bang theory. Some 15 billion years ago, the entire universe, all of space and time, was created in a single event. The event was a tremendous outrushing of matter and energy, like an explosion, that organized and reorganized itself into the universe we see today.

Support for this theory comes from many observations, including the discovery of a background temperature throughout the universe of about 3 degrees above absolute zero. The background temperature was first detected by radio telescopes in the 1960s and later confirmed by the *Cosmic Background Explorer* astronomy satellite. It appears to be the heat left over from the explosion. Another proof for the Big Bang is that most of the known galaxies in the known universe are moving away from one another. Their movement is something like the movements you would see if you drew ink dots on a round balloon and then inflated the balloon. If you could reverse the motions of all the galaxies, their paths would bring them together in one place. It would be like running a video of an explosion in reverse. The one place would be the site of the Big Bang.

tremendous surface gravity. If you weigh 50 kilograms (110 pounds on Earth) you would weigh 5,000,000,000,000 (trillion) kilograms (11,000,000,000,000 pounds) on a neutron star!

Neutron stars may be spinning very rapidly, and the light (radio waves) they give out spirals, or radiates, like the beam of a lighthouse. This makes them appear to pulse in the sky, and so they are called pulsars.

If the remnants of a red giant star have a mass three or more times greater than the mass of our Sun, they can become black holes. Their collapse is so great that they become infinitely small. This creates a gravitational pull so strong that light cannot escape from them—and that is why these stars are called black holes. If you could aim a flashlight beam past a black hole, the beam would turn as it neared the black hole and then disappear into it.

If black holes capture light, how can astronomers tell if they exist? The answer is that astronomers don't look directly for black holes but rather for the regions around black holes. If a black hole is near an ordinary star, the black hole's tremendous gravitational pull will yank matter away from the ordinary star. As the matter falls toward the black hole, it will spiral around it like water spirals around a sink drain. As it spirals into the black hole, friction causes the matter to heat up. Eventually, X-ray radiation is released from the spiral, and this can be detected by astronomy spacecraft. Several suspected black holes have been detected in this manner over the years, but recent *Hubble Space Telescope* images have actually shown the spiral around a few black holes.

QUASARS

In the 1960s, astronomers discovered very distant bright pinpoints of light that looked like stars. But because they were millions of light-years away and seemed to be moving outward at tremendous velocities, they had to be billions of times brighter than normal stars. Astronomers reasoned that the objects could not possibly be individual stars. Scientists called these mysterious bodies quasi-stellar objects, or quasars.

Astronomers have come to believe that quasars and black holes are related. Quasars are found in galaxies where supermassive black holes are present. If the black hole is large enough, the energy given off as matter spirals down into it can shoot off in narrow, searchlight beacons traveling in opposite directions. If you compare the spiral

This quasar is believed to result from a black hole residing very near a galaxy 1.5 billion light-years away. Debris falling into the black hole causes intense amounts of energy to be radiated outward. Eventually, the entire galaxy may be sucked into the black hole.

of a black hole to a compact disc (CD), the beacons would originate at the hole of the CD. One beacon would go up and the other go down. Thus black holes seem to be the engines that power quasars.

GALAXIES

Among the largest structures in the universe are the galaxies. Edwin P. Hubble first realized that galaxies were huge clusters of stars, ranging in size from small, containing tens of millions of stars, to behemoths with hundreds of billions of stars. What makes these star clusters galaxies is that the stars within them are tied to one another by gravity and revolve around one another. Hubble's studies led to a galaxy classification system and to a method for determining how far they are from Earth.

Galaxies take a few basic shapes, with many variations. The primary shapes are elliptical, spiral, and irregular. Elliptical galaxies range in shape from spheres to squashed-egg forms. They are home to many very old Sun-like stars, but little else. They have almost no visible gas or dust and are therefore unlikely to host stellar nurseries.

Spiral galaxies are characterized by a disk of stars that spirals around a large globular collection of stars called the nucleus. Our Milky Way galaxy is a spiral. Spirals have large quantities of gas and dust, and so they promote active star formation. One group of spirals has no obvious spiraling arms present. These galaxies have nuclei and a disk but have little gas and dust or very hot stars as other spirals do. Because of a lack of visible spiral arms, these galaxies could be intermediate stages between the elliptical and spiral galaxies. Another possible interpretation is that the spiral arms were stripped away during one or more collisions with other galaxies.

Another kind of spiral galaxy is the barred spiral. Its distinguishing feature is the elongation of the nucleus, so that it looks like a bar running through the galaxy.

Finally is the irregular galaxy, which has no special shape. Irregulars contain mixtures of star types and large clouds of gas and dust. Stars both young and old are present.

One of the current areas of galactic research is the effort to find an accurate way of measuring distances to galaxies. This is important because the method will tell astronomers what is happening to our universe. Edwin

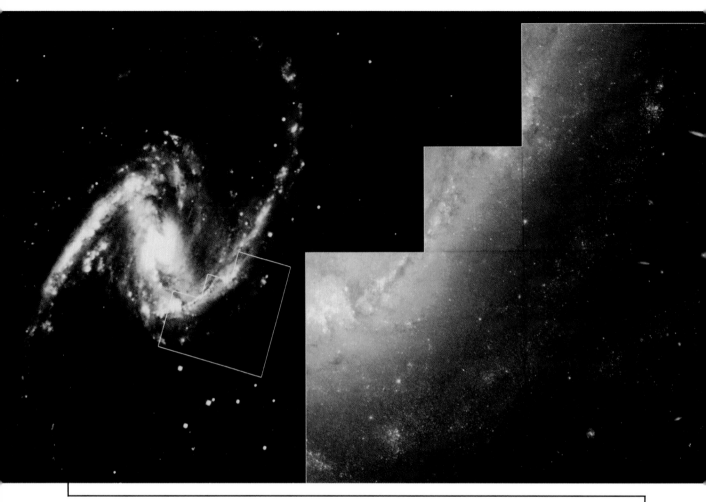

The black-and-white picture of galaxy NGC 1365 was taken with a ground-based telescope. A portion of the galaxy was looked at more closely with the *Hubble Space Telescope*. Bluish areas in the picture show where stars appear to be forming in the galaxy. This galaxy is believed to lie 60 million light-years away.

Hubble determined that galactic distance and velocity (speed) are related. The galaxies nearer to us are moving away more slowly than the distant galaxies. The relationship involves using a mathematical constant, just as pi is used in determining the circumference of a circle. The problem is knowing exactly how big the constant should be. This requires having some extremely accurate mea-

DEEP SPACE
ASTRONOMY

surements of several galaxies for comparison. Getting these measurements involves the *Hubble Space Telescope.*

Certain stars, called Cepheid variables, and certain supernovae are distinctive in the light they give out. If these kinds of stars can be identified in distant galaxies, the distance to them can be estimated. The technique is something like seeing a lightbulb burning outside a distant farmhouse. If you know the light comes from a 100-watt lightbulb, then you will know how bright it should be. The next step is to have some type of instrument that accurately tells you how bright the lightbulb appears from where you are standing. Let's say that you are 100 meters (328 feet) from the bulb, and you measure its brightness. Then you move to an unknown distance and measure the bulb's brightness again. This time it is about one-quarter as bright. That will tell you that you are twice as far away. If the bulb is only one-ninth as bright, you are three times farther away. The relationship is based on the inverse square law. In other words, if you square the distance to the light and then divide it into the number 1, you will know how bright the bulb will be. Quadruple your distance (4 squared equals 16) and divide it into the number 1 and you get one-sixteenth.

Astronomers have been using the *Hubble Space Telescope* to estimate the distance to several galaxies. Then they compare the distance to how fast the galaxies are moving away from us. This gives them a value for the constant. Making this kind of measurement is difficult, and the value of the constant is still not accurately known. When its value is set, the constant will be invaluable for determining the distance to galaxies that are too far away to detect by measuring the Cepheid variables and supernovae within the galaxies.

What is the point of accurate distances? Astronomers will be able to use this information and estimates for the amount of mass (all the galaxies, their stars, and other space debris combined) to determine the fate of our universe. At this time the universe is expanding. The galaxies are moving away from one another. Will they continue to spread apart forever, or will gravity cause them to stop and fall back into one another? The situation is like tossing a baseball upward. If you toss it fast enough, it will escape Earth's gravity and forever head outward into space. If you don't toss it fast enough, gravity will slow it down and cause it to fall back. If the galaxies continue moving apart, many billions of years from now the universe will thin out and slowly fade. If gravity stops the outward motion, the galaxies will fall back in on themselves, and the universe will start itself over in a cataclysmic explosion.

CHAPTER 4

DISCOVERY MACHINES: THE NEXT GENERATION

Each new space observatory launched above Earth helps astronomers answer questions about the objects found in, and the processes going on in, deep space. At the same time, these discovery machines reveal unexpected details that lead to new questions. So many new questions are created that the work of astronomers seems never ending. The fundamental questions that astronomers are asking today are many:

- How did the universe begin?

- What is the ultimate fate of the universe?

- How did galaxies, stars, and planets evolve?

• What kind of processes take place in extreme environments such as supernovae and black holes?

• How did life begin on Earth, and where else might it be found?

• What will happen to our Sun over time, and how will that affect Earth and the other planets?

• How might humans inhabit other worlds?

There are no simple answers to these questions. Each answer is extremely complicated and consists of many parts. It is like asking where rain comes from. Answering that it comes from the sky is only the beginning. A complete answer requires knowing what water is, where the water comes from, how it came to be in the sky, what conditions trigger rainfall, what happens to the raindrops as they fall, and where the rain goes after it falls. The fundamental questions about space need to be answered the same way.

As we have seen in earlier chapters, astronomers cannot conduct their experiments directly in a laboratory. Planets, stars, and galaxies do not fit into test tubes. Furthermore, the time frame for the creation and evolution of the universe stretches across billions of years. Compare this to the 40 years or so that an astronomer might have to conduct his or her work. Instead of direct experimentation, astronomers must rely on their instruments, peering across the vastness of space and collecting their data. In order to do that, they use both Earth-based telescopes and spacecraft. These scientists then interpret the data they have gathered based on their understanding of the electromagnetic spectrum.

Discovery machines such as the *Hubble Space Telescope* and the *Compton Gamma Ray Observatory* are complex devices that required many years of design and development before they were ready to be launched into space.

The process is exciting, but it is also frustrating. At some point, all those involved in the launching of these machines have to agree upon the final design of the spacecraft. Construction then begins, and only minor design changes, if any, are permitted. However, by the time each of these machines actually flies into space, the instruments on the spacecraft are obsolete. Newer and better instruments have already been designed. Astronomers have to resist the temptation to alter the spacecraft. Each new development would mean a delay, and the spacecraft might never get launched. To do its work the spacecraft has to be in space, even with somewhat outdated instruments on board.

Solutions to this problem include the strategy employed by the developers of the *Hubble Space Telescope*. The spacecraft was designed with orbital replacement units (ORUs) in mind. An ORU is an instrument or a spacecraft system that can be plugged into the structure of the telescope and later removed and replaced by something better. It is like having a home stereo system made of individual parts such as a tape deck, radio tuner, amplifier, and speakers. If the amplifier breaks down or a better one becomes available, the old one is removed and the new one is inserted. The ORU strategy is what made the *Hubble Space Telescope* such an important discovery machine. Two space shuttle crews have already visited the spacecraft and replaced solar panels, corrected optical problems, added new stabilizing devices, and replaced obsolete instruments with newer and more powerful ones. NASA is working on the changes that will be made to the spacecraft during the next shuttle visit. With this sort of updating and repair, the *Hubble Space Telescope* is expected to serve astronomers at least until the year 2010.

Another solution to the problem of spacecraft that become obsolete is to construct new spacecraft to replace or supplement the ones already operating in space. In other words, scientists must build the next generation of discovery machines. The *Next Generation Space Telescope* (*NGST*) is already on the drawing board, although important design details have to be worked out.

DEEP SPACE: THE NEXT GENERATION

Planned for launch in 2007, the *Next Generation Space Telescope* will have a mirror at least double the size of the one for the *Hubble Space Telescope*. The *NGST* will be able to collect four to eight times more light and see deeper into space than the *HST*.

Rather than placing the *Next Generation Space Telescope* in Earth orbit, plans call for it to be sent out to a stable place between Earth and the Sun almost four times farther away than the Moon is. The *NGST* will have an infrared instrument 1,000 times more sensitive than any used by other spacecraft. The instrument is so sensitive that even sunlight reflected back into space from Earth will affect it. The great distance from Earth will help keep the *NGST* cool enough to do its work.

The *Next Generation Space Telescope* isn't the only astronomy spacecraft being planned. Also in development is the *Far-Infrared and Submillimeter Telescope* that will look for galaxies that formed when the universe was less than a billion years old. The *Gamma-Ray Large Area Space Telescope* will look for gamma rays coming from massive black holes. The *Planck* mission, named after German physicist Max Planck, will study the microwave zone of the electromagnetic spectrum to look for dark matter in our galaxy. Astronomers believe that the universe has great quantities of material—dark matter—that does not give off visible light. One of the questions they have about the movement of the galaxies away from one another is whether gravity will eventually stop them and cause them to fall back. If dark matter exists, there will probably be enough gravity to stop the expansion. The *Planck* mission may answer the question. Finally, the *Roentgen Satellite* will map X rays from distant galaxies and supernova remnants. These and dozens of other planned space observatories will be collaborative efforts by the space agencies of many countries. They are being designed to answer today's questions about the universe—and to answer questions that haven't even been asked.

RECENT DISCOVERIES IN DEEP SPACE

With all the tools available to them, today's astronomers have come to realize that the universe is filled with bizarre objects and is home to odd, puzzling events. Daily, new discoveries are made that cause astronomers to rethink old ideas.

Without warning, bursts of gamma-ray radiation appear in small patches from different directions in the sky. One burst is detected each day by the *Compton Gamma Ray Observatory*. The bursts peak quickly and then fade away. Their source and what causes them are unknown. Only recently have astronomers been able to coordinate observations from different spacecraft and ground-based telescopes in hopes of solving the mystery. Now, when a burst is detected by the *CGRO*, other spacecraft and telescopes zero in on it. The combined observations have helped astronomers conclude that the bursts are being given off in titanic explosions of objects billions of light-years away from the Milky Way. One possible explanation of the bursts is that they result from the collisions of neutron stars.

At the core of the Milky Way, 25,000 light-years from Earth, a gigantic star was discovered by the *Hubble Space Telescope*. It is called the Pistol Star because of the pistol-shaped nebula nearby. This star is so huge that, were it to replace the Sun, the Earth, at its present distance from the Sun (150 million kilometers, or 93 million miles), would be swallowed up inside it. The Pistol Star is thought to be a relative youngster as stars go—only 1 to 3 million years old. When it formed, the star was perhaps the largest ever. Tremendous quantities of gas and other debris fell inward onto this star because of its gravitational attraction. It is believed that eventually the Pistol Star accumulated a mass 200 times greater than the mass of our Sun. Stars that size are thought to be highly unstable, and this star probably began to have surface explosions. Astronomers theorize that in the last 6,000 years, two explosions kicked matter the equivalent of several suns off the star's surface. Presently, the Pistol Star has a mass of about 100 suns. The shed material from the star now surrounds it in a great nebula.

Studies of our Sun, with the Japanese *Yohkoh* satellite and the NASA/European *SOHO* satellite, have led to some startling discoveries. For years, our Sun was thought to be an average star with a relatively quiet surface. There were sunspots and modest ejections of gas, but nothing like the ejections that occur with massive stars. Now a different picture emerges. Recent discoveries on the Sun include jet streams of hot gas, similar to but larger than the trade winds on Earth, running beneath its surface. The streams appear to snake around the Sun at a depth of about 20,000 kilometers (12,427 miles). The streams may play a role in the development of sunspots and gas ejections.

Also observed in the Sun are sunquakes that are about 40,000 times more powerful than the 1906 San Francisco earthquake, and tornadoes twisting across the solar surface. The quakes look like the wave patterns that occur when a pebble is tossed in a pond. The waves spread outward at initial speeds of 35,000 kilometers (21,748 miles) per hour and increase to speeds at least 10 times greater before dissipating. The Sun tornadoes, much larger than those on Earth, have rotary wind speeds up to 500,000 kilometers (310,686 miles) per hour. On Earth, tornadoes typically whirl across the planet's surface at speeds up to about 500 kilometers (310 miles) per hour.

The life and death of stars has always been a fascinating study, but never more so than now. Supernovae were once thought to be the greatest explosions that stars could undergo, but not anymore. Scientists now have evidence of a far-greater stellar explosion called a hypernova. In a single explosion, a hypernova may give off 100 times more energy than a typical supernova. After the outer layers of a star that has gone supernova have dissipated into space, the remainder of the star collapses into a neutron star. With the hypernova, the force of the explosion is so great that the remainder of the star may fall into itself and become a black hole. One of these hypernova stars was discovered in 1998. Measurements of the star's outward flow of energy by X-ray satellites and radio telescopes have indicated the force of the explosion was so great that the material expelled was traveling outward at 98 percent the speed of light.

DEEP SPACE:
THE NEVER
ENDING STORY

Deep space holds mysteries that have fascinated humans for thousands of years. Its secrets have only begun to be probed. With space observatories, the pace of discovery has accelerated. Each new discovery has led to new questions, which have led to new searches, which have led to more new discoveries. It is an exciting time to be an astronomer because there is so much to do and so much to learn.

We have learned that the universe is one great family of stars. Stars are clustered in galaxies, and some stars are almost as ancient as the universe itself, while others are only a few million years old. There are giant stars and stars smaller than Earth. Looking into space is like looking into a family album containing trillions of members, each with its own story. We are a part of that story. We live on a planet that orbits a star that belongs to a galaxy. Our story is that of life and wonder. One of our great questions is: Are we alone? We do not know the answer to that yet, but it seems unlikely that the only living things in our vast and varied universe are found on a single planet.

We know that other planets are orbiting our star, but are there planets orbiting other stars? Astronomers have detected stars with a peculiar wobble. The stars move about as though an unseen body, a large planet, were circling them. Until recently, no picture of a planet orbiting another star had ever been taken. Once again, the *Hubble Space Telescope* changed all that. In a dusty region in the direction of the constellation Taurus, the image of a planet was captured. The planet, about two or three times the mass of Jupiter, is spinning out of orbit from a star 450 light-years away from Earth. The planet appears to be trailing a long column of dust that was kicked away from the star when the planet was ejected. The picture, taken by the *HST*, is the first ever of a planet outside our solar system.

Galaxies, stars, nebulae, and planets: Our universe beckons us with trillions of stories waiting to be told.

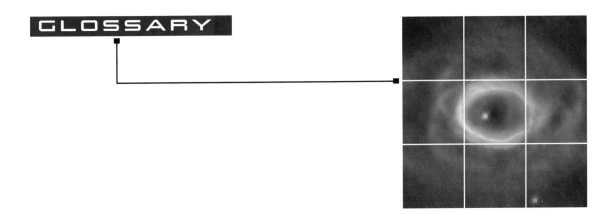

absolute zero   the coldest that matter can become: –273°C (–460°F)

barred spiral galaxy   a spiral galaxy that has a barlike structure of stars running through its middle

Big Bang   the initial expansion of the universe

black dwarf   an Earth-size star that no longer gives off light

black hole   a massive star that has collapsed upon itself and whose gravity is so intense that even light cannot escape from it

Cepheid variable   a star that varies in brightness as the result of regular changes in its size and temperature

crest   the highest part of a wave

dark matter   invisible matter in space that is detectable only by the gravitational pull it exerts on visible objects around it

diameter   the distance across a circle or sphere

electromagnetic spectrum   all known forms of radiation, from radio waves to gamma radiation

elliptical galaxy   a galaxy that has an elliptical or squashed-egg shape

evaporating gaseous globules (EGGs)   spherical gas clouds in which stars are forming

freezing point of water   0°C (32°F)

frequency   the number of waves passing a reference point in one second

galaxy   a huge collection of stars (millions to hundreds of billions), gas, and dust connected to one another by gravity

hypergiant   a star at least 1,000 times larger than the Sun

irregular galaxy   a galaxy with no defined shape

light-year   the distance that light travels in one year's time

Milky Way galaxy   the spiral galaxy in which we reside

National Aeronautics and Space Administration (NASA)   the agency of the United States government that is charged with exploring the atmosphere and space

nebula   a cloud of gas and dust in space that may be lit up by the light of nearby stars

neutron   a particle found in the nucleus or center of an atom that does not have an electric charge

neutron star   a very small star, only about 10 kilometers (6 miles) in diameter, composed only of atomic particles called neutrons

nova   an explosion on a star that ejects a layer of gas

Orbital Replacement Units (ORUs)   scientific instruments and spacecraft systems that are designed to be replaced by spacewalking astronauts

phases   changes in the shape of a planet or the Moon because of the amount of reflected sunlight and shadows we see

planetary nebula   a shell of gas surrounding a star that looks like a planet through low-power telescopes

quasar   a pinpoint of light as powerful as billions of stars that possibly originates from matter falling into a black hole

radius   the distance from the center of a circle or sphere to its outer edge

speed of light   299,792 kilometers (186,282 miles) per second

sphere a ball-shaped object having all points on its surface equally distant from its center

spiral galaxy a galaxy in which many of the stars are arranged in spiral arms that stretch outward from the galaxy's center

star a great ball of hot gas held together by its own gravity

supernova the explosive destruction of a star

super red giant a star as large as Earth's orbit that gives off red light

trough the low point in a wave

universe stars, planets, galaxies, and everything else that exists throughout space

visible light the part of the electromagnetic spectrum that we can see

wavelength the length of a wave from one wave crest (or trough) to the next wave crest (or next trough)

white dwarf an Earth-size remnant of a star that is hot enough to give off white light

SPACE OBSERVATORIES

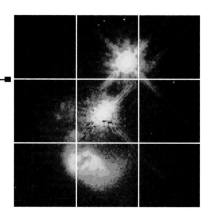

Chandra X-Ray Observatory (CXF)
a NASA space observatory that will collect X-ray radiation

Compton Gamma Ray Observatory (CGRO)
a NASA space observatory that collects gamma radiation

Cosmic Background Explorer (COBE)
a space observatory that measured the background radiation of the universe and found that the temperature of space is about 2.7 degrees Celsius above absolute zero

Far-Infrared and Submillimeter Telescope
a European-sponsored mission to study infrared radiation

Gamma-Ray Large Area Space Telescope
a future gamma-ray telescope

Hubble Space Telescope (HST)   a NASA space observatory that primarily collects visible light

Infrared Astronomical Satellite (IRAS)   an old NASA space observatory that collected infrared radiation

Next Generation Space Telescope (NGST)
a new space telescope planned for launch in 2007

Planck   a European-sponsored mission to study microwave radiation

Roentgen Satellite   a planned X-ray satellite

Space Infrared Telescope Facility (SIRTF)
a NASA space observatory that will collect infrared radiation

MAJOR ASTRONOMY MISSIONS

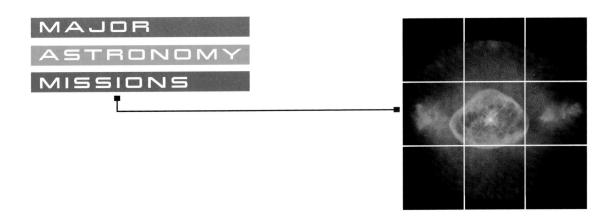

(PARTIAL LIST)

YEAR	MISSION	TARGET	HIGHLIGHTS
1957	*Stratoscope I*	Sun	Balloon launch, sponsored by Princeton University
1961	*Explorer 11*	gamma rays	62 days, first look at gamma rays from space
1962	*Arobee*	X-ray sources	First X-ray source outside solar system: Sco-X-1
1967	*OSO-3*	gamma rays	Detected gamma rays from Milky Way
1968	*RAE-1*	cosmic radio noise	Looked at cosmic radio noise
1968	*OAO-2*	ultraviolet light	Studied ultraviolet radiation from the Sun
1969	*Vela 5A*	gamma rays	Detected gamma rays from space

YEAR	MISSION	TARGET	HIGHLIGHTS
1970	*SAS-1*	X-ray sky	Renamed *Uhuru (Explorer 42)*; studied the X-ray sky
1971	*Explorer 43*	solar wind/cosmic radio noise	Monitored solar wind and cosmic radio noise
1972	*Copernicus*	ultraviolet	Operated for nine years; last *OAO*
1973	*Skylab*	major solar mission	Crewed mission that included study of the Sun
1973	*Explorer 49*	radio sources	*RAE-2* in lunar orbit monitored radio sources
1975	*SAS-3*	X-ray sources	*SAS*-3 launched—*Explorer 53*—determined positions of X-ray sources
1978	*IUE*	ultraviolet sky	In use until 1996
1978	*HEAO-2*	X-ray sky	Renamed *Einstein*; studied X-ray sky
1983	*IRAS*	infrared	US–Dutch 300-day mission to observe universe in the infrared
1989	*COBE*	microwave sky	Launched from a *Delta* rocket to study the microwave sky. Detected remnant radiation from the Big Bang